KU-205-002

DONCASTER LIBRARY AND INFORMATION SERVICE		
3O122O2159547 1		
Askews	10-Mar-2005
J608	£7.99

This edition published 2005 by
Mercury Books
20 Bloomsbury Street
London WC1B 3JH
ISBN 1-904668-73-9

Copyright © 2003 Allegra Publishing Ltd

Publisher: Felicia Law
Design director: Tracy Carrington
Project manager: Karen Foster
Author: Gerry Bailey
Editor: Rosalind Beckman
Designed by: Jacqueline Palmer
assisted by Fanny Level, Will Webster
Cartoon illustrations: Steve Boulter (Advocate)
and Andrew Keylock (Specs Art Agency)
Make-and-do: Jan Smith
Model-maker: Tim Draper
further models: Robert Harvey, Abby Dean
Photo studio: Steve Lumb
Photo research: Diana Morris
Scanning: Acumen Colour
Digital workflow: Edward MacDermott

Printed by D 2 Print Singapore

Photo Credits
AKG Images: 5t, 13t. Bob Battersby/Eye Ubiquitous: 22b.
Bettmann/Corbis: 21t, 37t, 41t. C/B Production/Corbis: 26b.
James Davis Travel Photography: 9t. Chris Fairclough/Eye Ubiquitous: 10b.
Jon Feingersh/Corbis: 33t. I. Joannopolous/MIT/SPL: 34b.
Mura/Jerrican/SPL:38b.
NASA: 17t, 29t, 30b. Photri/Topham: 18b.
Roger Ressmeyer/Corbis: 42b. Nancy Richmond/The Image
Works/Topham: 14b.
Marcus Stace/Eye Ubiquitous: 25t. Allan Tannenbaum/The Image
Works/Topham:6b.

INTO THE FUTURE

Contents

Mercury Junior

20 BLOOMSBURY STREET
LONDON WC1B 3JH

How can I power a horseless carriage?

Karl has always been interested in engineering and transport. He wants to find a new method of transport that doesn't use horses. In fact, he's looking to build a horseless carriage. But what kind of alternative power can he use?

Nicolas Cugnot used steam to power a carriage in 1769. But his steam machine was awkward and slow, and crashed after just 20 minutes. Other steam carriages have been built since then, but they are noisy and smoky, and they frighten animals. There has to be a better way.

What can I use instead of horse power?

Karl does not like the idea of using electricity. Although carriages that use it are quiet, they are slow and the batteries do not last.

WHAT CAN HE DO?

- Attaching a mast and sails to his carriage might do it. But passengers would be at a standstill on a calm day.

- What about an electric car with a long lead? It wouldn't run out of electricity, but it wouldn't go very far, either.

- He could use an internal combustion engine that burns some sort of liquid fuel. Now that would be easier to carry.

- How about using Etienne Lenoir's 1860 engine? It powered machines such as printing presses and water pumps. But it was noisy and not very efficient.

I'll modify an internal combustion engine. It can sit at the back of my carriage and I'll attach it to the back wheels by a chain. Then I'll have one wheel in front that I can steer with a handle.

Benz's first automobile had three wheels. His rival, Gottlieb Daimler, made the first four-wheel car.

Combustion engine

An **automobile** is a road vehicle. It is usually powered by an **internal combustion engine**, which produces power by burning petrol and air in a series of **cylinders**. Most automobiles burn petrol, but some burn diesel fuel or liquid gas. In 1885, Karl Benz and Gottlieb Daimler, working independently, developed the first useful **four-stroke engine**, in which the **pistons** in the cylinders go through a series of four movements or strokes. Cars tend to use similar engines today. In 1891, a French company, Panhard et Levassor, created a car with an engine in front that turned the rear wheels. Many cars were designed that way until front-wheel drive became popular.

Petrol

Petrol is a liquid fuel that is made from petroleum, or crude oil. Petroleum is a dark liquid that is found beneath the Earth's surface. It is a **fossil fuel** because it is made from the bodies of plants and animals that died millions of years ago.

Petroleum is refined, or made more pure, to produce petrochemicals, lubricants such as the oils used to lubricate engines, and fuel such as petrol. The refining is done in a special factory called a **refinery**. During the refining process, impure substances such as sulphur and hydrogen are removed from the petroleum. Once it is ready, the petrol is pumped along pipes to large holding areas. It is then taken by tanker to petrol stations. A pump at the station is used to pump petrol into cars, trucks, buses and other road vehicles.

AFFORDABLE CARS

The first cars were hand-built, which took a long time and made them expensive. This method changed when Henry Ford introduced the assembly line.

His Model Ts moved along the line from one group of workers to another. From then on, cars became affordable for ordinary people.

Oil gushes out of an oil well in Kuwait.

Inventor's words

automobile
internal combustion
engine • cylinder
fossil fuel
four-stroke engine
petrol • piston
refinery

Brmm! Brmm!

Make your own push-car

You will need

- chicken wire • newspaper
- PVA glue • plastic bottles
- sticky tabs • straws
- double-sided sticky tape
- cardboard • thin card
- kebab sticks • foil cases
- paints and brush

1 Make a car frame out of chicken wire. Cover with strips of newspaper soaked in a half-water, half-PVA glue solution.

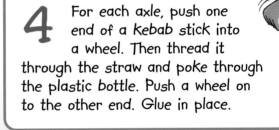

2 Cut a plastic bottle in half. Fix each half to the underside of the car with sticky tabs, then secure with wire, as shown. Make holes in the sides of each bottle and push a straw through each one. Tape to fix.

3 Cut 8 discs of cardboard. Divide into 4 pairs and glue together. Cover 4 long strips of thin card with double-sided tape, then lay around each pair of discs to form a thick wheel.

4 For each axle, push one end of a kebab stick into a wheel. Then thread it through the straw and poke through the plastic bottle. Push a wheel on to the other end. Glue in place.

5 Glue on the foil cases to make wheel hubs. Then paint your car in bright colours.

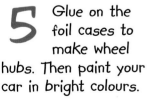

How can I build up rather than out?

Towns and cities are growing. Buildings take up a lot of space and land is expensive. Some people believe it would be cheaper to construct tall buildings that can house a lot of people without taking up much room on the ground. But there is a danger that they might topple over.

The city of Chicago is getting larger by the day as business grows and more people want to live there. William is an architect who can *see* that the problem of space would be solved if he could construct a tall building instead of a wide one.

How can I make a tower that won't topple?

But tall buildings can *be* a problem. Unless they are built solidly, they will fall down. They also have to withstand strong winds or even earthquakes. Somehow, they need to be anchored to the ground.

WHAT CAN HE DO?

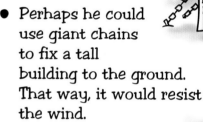

- Perhaps he could use giant chains to fix a tall building to the ground. That way, it would resist the wind.

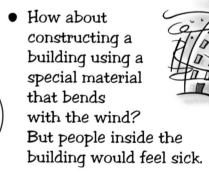

- How about constructing a building using a special material that bends with the wind? But people inside the building would feel sick.

- If he used a very heavy material at the bottom of the building, it would provide a firm base. But the rest of the building might still fall over.

- He could dig a large hole in the ground and start the base of the building there. That might make it secure, but the framework of the building would still be weak.

I'll make a deep hole into which I can *build* a *secure base*, or foundation. On top of that I'll build a frame of *steel girders* to carry the weight of the building's walls and roof.

At 452m high, the world's tallest building is the Petronas Towers in Kuala Lumpur. It has 81 stories, with a link on the 41st floor.

Tall towers

A **skyscraper** is a tall building with many storeys. Most skyscrapers are built on **frames** made of steel **girders**, or beams, that carry the weight of the building. The first skyscraper built in this way was the 42m-high, Home Insurance Building in Chicago, USA, designed by the American architect William Jenney, and built in 1885.

Skyscrapers have two main sections: the **foundations**, the part below ground; and the **superstructure**, the part above ground. Both sections help support the weight, called the **load**, of the building. When skyscrapers are over 40 storeys, high wind load becomes more important than the weight of the building.

Loads

A load is a weight. It is the weight that a force pushes against. Beams and bridges support loads. Engineers and architects who construct, or build, skyscrapers talk about the load of the building instead of its weight.

In low buildings – buildings of four storeys or less – the load is transmitted, or moved, to the foundations. Strong foundations take the weight of the walls and roof, and stop the building from falling down. Skyscrapers cannot be built just with foundations. They need a different method of construction. Skyscrapers must be built with a steel or concrete frame inside. This supports the load of the building, just like our skeleton supports us. The walls do not transmit loads but hang on the frame. The frame carries the loads of the walls, roof and floors.

TOWER CRANES

Tower cranes are used to lift heavy beams and other equipment needed to build a skyscraper. The crane is supported on a steel tower, so it can only hoist material from close by. Sections can be added to the crane to make it higher as the building goes up.

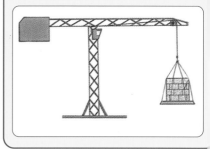

Steel beams and girders a bolted together to build t frame of a skyscraper.

Inventor's words

foundation
frame
girder
load
skyscraper
superstructure

Make a skyscraper

You will need

- thick card
- pencil • ruler
- shallow cardboard box
- yoghurt pots
- plastic bottles
- straws
- paint • paintbrush
- scissors • glue

1 Make a rectangular column from thick card.

2 Mark off the storeys at regular intervals up the column. Draw in some standard features, such as doors, stairs, a lift and entrances.

3 Cut out an oblong piece of card, then cut a hole in it for the card column to fit through. Use this as a template for making as many floors as you like. Cut flaps into the lift shaft hole on each floor, as shown. Now decorate each floor in a different colour.

4 Insert small supports made from card at the 4 corners of each floor. You can also stick paper walls on to 2 sides of the building.

5 Construct a roof spire from bottles, pots and straws. Spray with silver paint and glue to the top of your skyscraper.

How tall can you make your building?

How can I talk to someone far away?

Alexander works with deaf people. He's interested in how people hear and how sound travels through the air. He knows that people can only talk or shout to each other over a limited distance. After that the sound disappears.

Alexander understands that when we speak, we create sound waves, or tiny vibrations in the air. These sound waves are picked up by a listener's ear. The vibrations cause the eardrum to vibrate and signals are sent to the brain to tell us what the sound is. But, like ripples in a pond, sound waves die out over a short distance.

> How can I make sound travel a long way?

If there was a way to make the waves travel further, people could communicate over longer distances. Perhaps the sound waves need to be amplified, or made bigger. Or even changed into something else.

WHAT CAN HE DO?

- A giant megaphone to make the sound of his voice louder might help. But the megaphone would be much too big to carry around - and might deafen people close by.

- What if he made a special kind of telegraph with a transmitter and receiver?

- The device can still only send telegraph messages. But when the receiver is hit, he can hear sounds.

- The vibration of the telegraph causes variations in the electric current, which, in turn, cause variations in the receiver. Vibrations are important.

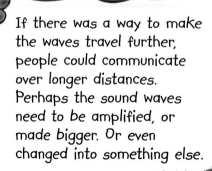

I'll make a transmitter with a vibrating membrane. I'll attach the transmitter by wire to a receiver that also has a membrane. Sound will make the transmitter's membrane vibrate and cause changes in the electric current. This will make the receiver's membrane vibrate and duplicate the sound.

Alexander Graham Bell demonstrates his first telephone in 1876. He used a hole in a box both to speak through and to listen.

Telephone connection

A **telephone** is an instrument for communicating over a distance or out of the hearing range of another person. When someone speaks into the mouthpiece of a telephone, the sounds cause a thin metal disc, or **diaphragm**, to vibrate. At the same time, a steady current of electricity passes through part of the mouthpiece.

The electric current is changed by the vibration of the diaphragm. This altered current then travels through a series of wires to the person receiving the call. Here the electric current makes a diaphragm in the listener's earpiece vibrate. This diaphragm duplicates the original sound so it is heard as it was spoken.

Electric charge

An **atom** is a tiny speck of **matter**. It is made up of a **nucleus**, or middle part, and **electrons** that move around in an orbit. The nucleus is made up of tinier **particles** called **protons** and **neutrons**. Protons have a positive electric charge. Electrons have a negative electric charge. Neutrons, as their name suggests, are neutral – they have no electric charge at all.

Like the positive and negative ends of bar magnets, electrons and protons attract each other. That is why the electrons stay in orbit. In some materials such as copper, however, there are free electrons that just float around.

NUCLEAR REACTION

Scientists discovered that when the nucleus of an atom is split, huge amounts of energy are suddenly released. If this happens quickly, it causes a massive nuclear explosion; if it happens slowly, the energy can be used to create electricity.

They are not part of an atom. A power source such as a battery makes these electrons move along a copper wire from the negative terminal to the positive terminal. This flow of electrons makes an electric current, like the one in Bell's telephone. In the telephone, each sound alters the flow of electrons in a certain way, so a message can be sent along the wire to the receiver.

The changes in an electric current allow people to speak to, and hear each other, on the telephone.

Inventor's words

atom • diaphragm
electron • matter
neutron • nucleus
particle • proton
telephone

Make your string-and-pot phone

You will need

- clean yoghurt pots
- string • paint
- brush
- chopsticks

1 Take 2 large yoghurt pots and puncture a small hole in the base of each one.

2 Using a long piece of string, push one end through the bottom of each pot. Tie a double knot inside to secure.

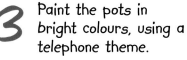

3 Paint the pots in bright colours, using a telephone theme.

4 Decorate 2 chopsticks with string and paint to make strikers.

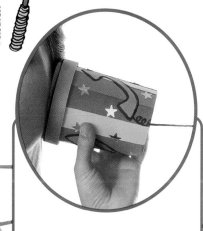

TO CALL A FRIEND

Each of you should hold a pot to your ear, pulling the string taut between you. To begin a conversation, tap the string with your striker – this will send a vibration down the line – then start talking.

How can we travel by air?

Men have already flown in the air, but only by balloon. However, a balloon cannot be steered. If people are going to fly, they will want to choose where they are going. That means using a power source and wings. But how is it possible to combine the two?

Orville and Wilbur Wright make bicycles. They are also interested in flight. They know that to fly, they must make a machine with wings that work in the same way as a bird's wings. The wings will allow a machine that is heavier than air to fly.

We'll have to create a powered machine with bird-like wings.

The wings won't work by themselves. There must be some way of powering them. When the wings are pushed forward, they will rise up. But what can the brothers use to power their winged craft?

WHAT CAN THEY DO?

- How about making a huge pair of feather-covered wings and finding someone strong enough to flap them?

- Or constructing wooden wings and attaching them to people's arms? If they jumped off a building, they'd glide for a bit - but they'd also break their necks!

- Perhaps they could build a winged carriage and attach a bicycle pedal system to it. But the rider would need to peddle very quickly to flap the wings.

- A better idea would be an engine of some sort. But it would have to push the machine, rather than flap the wings.

We'll use a recent invention called a petrol engine. The engine will power a propeller that will push the aircraft. We'll make double wings out of lightweight material. The pilot will lie between the main wings to steer the craft.

Orville made the first-ever powered flight at Kitty Hawk, North Carolina, on 17 December 1903. It lasted 12 seconds.

Propelled skywards

An **aeroplane** is a heavier-than-air aircraft that has **wings** and is powered by an engine. The wings of an aeroplane are specially shaped to make the aircraft rise when it is in motion. An engine provides **thrust**, or forward movement. The first aeroplanes used petrol engines that turned a **propeller**. A propeller has two or more blades fixed to a shaft.

When the blades rotate, they create a thrust that pushes the aeroplane forwards. As aeroplanes were developed, more engines were added. Today, it is not unusual to have two on each wing. In modern aeroplanes, propeller engines have been replaced by jet engines, which are much more powerful. Today, all large aircraft are designed to keep flying even if one of the engines fails.

Wing-shapes

Wings are the part of an aircraft that make them fly. Aeroplane wings, like bird's wings, have to be a special shape. They are curved on the top and straight underneath.

The curved top of the wing is longer than the straight bottom. This means that the air moving over it has to move faster than the air moving under it, in order to join up at the back edge of the wing. Air is a gas. The faster a gas moves, the less pressure, or push it creates. So the faster-moving air on top of the wing pushes down less hard than the slower-moving air underneath it. As the push on top of the wing decreases, the push upwards lifts the aeroplane until it leaves the ground. As long as the aeroplane keeps moving fast enough, the wings will keep it in the air.

UPSIDE-DOWN WINGS

Racing cars use wings on the front and at the back. But they are upside down - the curved part is on the bottom. This means that the pressure comes from the top, pushing the wing and car down. This gives the car more grip.

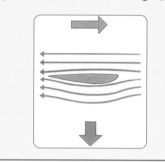

Wings can lift a heavy passenger plane off the ground when it reaches a certain speed.

Inventor's words

aeroplane
propeller
thrust • wing

Make a bottle propeller plane

You will need

- plastic drinks bottle
- kebab stick
- plastic sheet
- thick card
- large elastic bands
- soft wire • strong glue
- bottom half of another bottle

1 Make 2 holes in the bottom of the bottle with a kebab stick. Cut a propeller-shape from the plastic. Cut out 2 squares, 2 tail pieces, 3 discs and a wing shape from the card. Slit the tail pieces and wing flaps, as shown.

2 Loop a piece of elastic at both ends, then twist a piece of wire around one loop. Push the wire through the middle of the propeller, then through one piece of card and the bottle lid. Bend the wire down and glue on the other piece of card. Dangle the free end of the elastic inside the bottle and push the kebab stick through the loop and bottle to fix.

3 Glue the half bottle over the end of the first bottle to complete the body. Slit at one end, fix the tail pieces together and slot in.

4 Make the front and rear wheels by pushing wire through the bottom of the bottle and attaching the card discs.

5 Push another kebab stick through the front of the plane. Strap the wing panel to the body by twisting elastic bands around the 4 sticks.

Wind up the propeller by twisting it round with your finger. Let go and it will spin, pushing the plane forward.

19

How can I make moving pictures?

John knows that electric signals can be used to produce sounds. He is sure that they could also be used to produce moving pictures. The problem is how to change electricity into particles of light that people will see as moving pictures.

Moving pictures can *be seen* at a cinema. But John wants to create a machine that will show moving pictures in everyone's home. It would be like radio, but with live images shown on a screen. A cinema-type movie machine just wouldn't work.

How can I transmit live pictures?

LIVE

Movies only show what has been filmed. John wants to be able to show things as they are actually happening. He needs a kind of camera, or transmitter – one that does not need film.

WHAT CAN HE DO?

- What if he attached a battery to a pen to see if the pen drew a picture when the current was turned on? Very unlikely!

- How about sending radio waves? They can also carry electric signals. If only he could find a way to turn a scene into a series of radio signals.

- Studying the work of Campbell Swinton, a brilliant engineer, might help. He was on the right track with his modern scanning ideas.

- Perhaps he could scan the pictures he wanted to send. But he needs to make a machine to do this and also send the signals as radio waves.

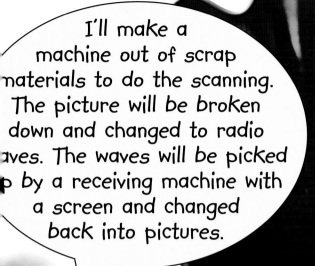

> I'll make a machine out of scrap materials to do the scanning. The picture will be broken down and changed to radio waves. The waves will be picked up by a receiving machine with a screen and changed back into pictures.

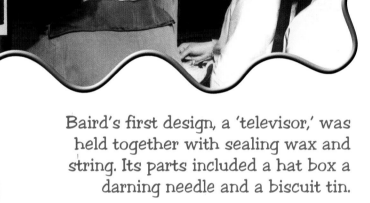

Baird's first design, a 'televisor,' was held together with sealing wax and string. Its parts included a hat box a darning needle and a biscuit tin.

Pictures on screen

Television is a method of sending and receiving sounds and pictures over a distance. It uses radio waves to carry electric signals through the atmosphere. British inventor, John Logie Baird, produced a black-and-white television image in 1926. At about the same time in America, Vladimir Zworykin was working on a different system.

Baird's system used spinning discs to record and display pictures, while Zworykin's was completely electronic. Zworykin created the first electronic camera, called an iconoscope. He also made an early version of the television picture tube, the kinescope. Colour programmes were broadcast in 1954 in America, and in 1967 in Europe.

Electron gun

An **electron** is a tiny **particle**, or speck, of **matter**. Electrons spin around the **nucleus**, or middle part, of an **atom**, just like planets orbit the Sun. Atoms are so small that one grain of sand will contain millions of them. If an atom is heated up, its electrons can be released to make a stream of electrons.

In a television, an **electron gun** shoots a very sharp beam of electrons at a **phosphorescent** screen. The screen is covered with a layer of **phosphors**, or solid chemicals, that glow when they are hit by the beam. When the electron beam hits the screen, it 'writes' the picture in lines of different levels of brightness, just like a pencil writing on paper. The more powerful the beam, the brighter the glow. The gun writes several hundred horizontal lines for each picture, and writes a line in a 60-millionth of a second. The lines make up the picture you see.

SHOOTING COLOUR

A colour television has three electron guns that fire through a metal grill behind the screen. The grill has rows of holes in it. The phosphors on the screen are arranged in groups of three, and glow green, blue or red, depending on which of the three electron beams hits them. The mix of glows gives us a true colour.

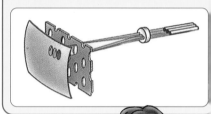

Inventor's words

atom • electron
electron gun
iconoscope
kinescope
matter • nucleus
particle • phosphor
phosphorescent
television

Electron guns are at the heart of many electronic machines, including the television.

Make your own flickerscope

You will need

- postal tube
- cardboard
- cane • stiff white card
- felt tip pens
- strong glue • sticky tape
- kebab stick • cork
- elastic bands
- lengh of wire
- plastic margerine tub

1 Cut off part of a postal tube to make the central drum. Stick cardboard discs at both ends. Push a cane through the centre.

2 Take 50 rectangles of stiff card and draw a simple picture on the first. Progress the image by drawing small changes on each card, to produce the effect of movement. Colour with felt tip pens.

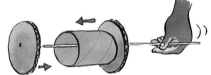

3 Score and fold each card 10mm along the bottom edge. Tape the cards to the drum, spacing them evenly around it. Glue between each image to fix.

4 Fit the drum into a cut-out box, as shown. Make a handle by attaching a kebab stick and cork to one end with an elastic band.

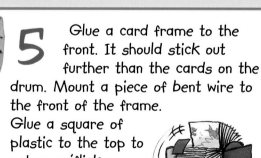

5 Glue a card frame to the front. It should stick out further than the cards on the drum. Mount a piece of bent wire to the front of the frame. Glue a square of plastic to the top to act as a 'flicker finger'. It should hold each picture card back slightly.

Turn the handle and let your movie pictures roll!

How can I make a tiny circuit?

Scientists working on military equipment want smaller and lighter electronic devices. Tiny switches called transistors, that change the strength of an electric current in a circuit, have helped. But the circuits are still too big for spacecraft or military equipment.

Jack knows that an electric circuit is the only way to get electricity to the parts that power an electronic device. Circuits made of wires are bulky, though.

Transistors reduce the size of computers and other equipment. But the scientists want even smaller devices.

How can I make a mini power plant?

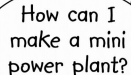

Space technology is growing. It takes a lot of components, including computers, to make a spacecraft work. Right now the components are bulky and expensive. They have to be made much smaller.

WHAT CAN HE DO?

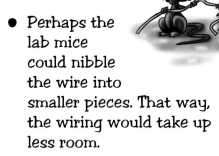

- Perhaps the lab mice could nibble the wire into smaller pieces. That way, the wiring would take up less room.

- Fixing a circuit on to a board might be better. It would be sturdy, but would it be small enough?

- He could find a way to make transistors even smaller, but he needs a special kind of material.

- A semiconductor material would be good. It conducts electricity better than materials like glass, although not as well as copper. So it makes a good circuit switch, or amplifier.

Silicon is a great semiconductor. It can be made much smaller than ordinary transistors and used as tiny sheets. I can place a mini circuit on to a tiny sheet, or chip, of silicon sunk into a plastic base.

Silicon chips are encased in a ceramic material with lots of metal 'pins' sticking out. This helps fix them on to a circuit board.

Miniature circuits

A **silicon chip** is also known as an **integrated circuit**. It is a miniature electronic circuit that is placed on a small piece of **silicon**. This circuit includes many tiny parts and wires. The piece of silicon is sunk into a plastic base. The chip can be very tiny – sometimes less than 4mm square.

Each chip is designed to do a particular job in an electronic device. Integrated circuits caused a revolution in electronics in the 1960s. They were first used in military equipment and spacecraft. Without them, the first manned space missions would not have been possible.

Semiconductors

A semiconductor is a type of solid material. It does not allow electricity to pass through it easily. But it does conduct electricity better than an insulator – a material that stops the flow of electricity – such as glass or rubber.

Semiconductor material includes germanium, selenium and lead sulphide, but the most often used is silicon. Silicon is a grey-coloured chemical **element**, a simple substance that contains only one kind of **atom**. It is the second most common element after oxygen, and is easily found in the Earth's crust. Silicon chips can be used to strengthen weak electric signals or change the kind of current used. Radios, televisions, computers and other electronic machines depend on semiconductors.

ARSENIC IN SEMICONDUCTORS

In conductors such as copper wire, the copper atoms have electrons that can move from atom to atom. This makes an electric current. Pure semi-conductor material has no free electrons. But when a substance such as arsenic is added, a few free electrons are produced.

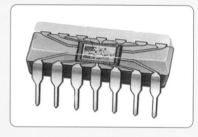

Circuit board for a computer.

Inventor's words

atom • element
electron
insulator
integrated circuit
semiconductor
silicon
silicon chip

Design a circuit board

You will need

- bottle, tin and pen tops, large plastic lids
- plastic tubs • sweet tray
- small yoghurt pots
- small cardboard boxes, e.g. egg cartons, matchboxes
- cardboard • PVA glue
- coloured card
- kebab sticks • tin foil
- silver paint • brush
- wire

1 Glue cardboard shapes on to a large piece of stiff cardboard.

2 Stick various plastic tubs, lids and small boxes into place.

3 Add bottle and pen tops and strips of coloured card.
Join up the components with kebab sticks.

4 Decorate with tin foil, silver paint and pieces of wire to look like a circuit board.

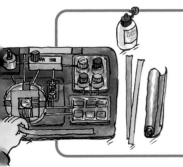

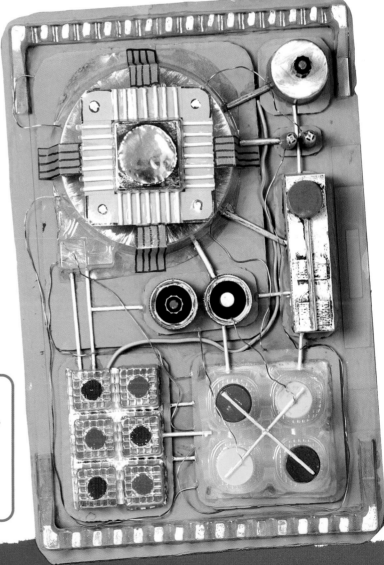

How can I propel a rocket sky high?

People talk about travelling to the Moon. But how can they get there? Some people think the best kind of power might be the rocket power developed by the Chinese around 1100. They used gunpowder - but that would not be powerful enough to send a rocket to the Moon.

Robert knows that the problem of powering a rocket a long way is the huge amount of fuel it will use. A rocket powered by gunpowder would have to be gigantic if it were to get anywhere near the Moon.

What type of fuel can I use to propel a rocket into space?

A rocket also needs to be powerful enough to break out of the Earth's atmosphere. The gravity of the Earth will be another problem. It will try to pull the craft back to the ground.

WHAT CAN HE DO?

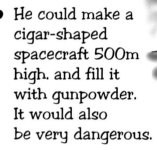

- He could make a cigar-shaped spacecraft 500m high. and fill it with gunpowder. It would also be very dangerous.

- How about a saucer-shaped craft with internal combustion engines around the edge? It would have power, but would it be aerodynamic?

- The cigar shape is best. He could add fins for stability and use a more effective fuel in the rocket engine.

- Perhaps he could replace the solid fuels with something else, such as gas or liquid fuel?

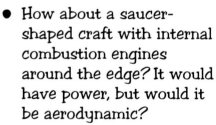

Liquid fuel will burn more efficiently when oxygen is added to it. It will give a better explosion and more power. I think I'll use liquid fuel in my new rocket and see how far it travels.

Goddard's rocket climbed 56m before falling into his aunt's backyard.

Upward thrust

A **rocket** is a device powered by explosive gases. Chemicals such as nitrogen in liquid form are mixed with oxygen to produce the gas. When they are heated, the gases **expand**, or take up more space, very quickly. This produces a strong force that **thrusts**, or pushes, the rocket upwards or forwards. The first rockets were invented by the Chinese nearly 1000 years ago.

During the 1800s, Colonel William Congreve of the British army developed rockets that carried explosives. These military rockets used solid fuel and travelled up to 2.4km. In 1926, Robert Goddard successfully launched a liquid-fuelled rocket. This was the beginning of the rocket and Space Age. Then, in 1961, Yuri Gagarin became the first person to travel in space.

Rocket power

A rocket motor is an engine that works by burning fuel and expelling, or pushing out, gases at high pressure. It contains pumps and other devices to control the burning of the fuel. Rocket motors are the most powerful kind of engine ever built.

A modern rocket carries tanks of fuel, such as liquid nitrogen and liquid oxygen. They are mixed and burned in a **combustion**, or burning, chamber. The result is an enormous amount of pressure and heat. Exhaust gases are blown out towards the ground through nozzles. As these gases blow down, the rocket is pushed up.

NEWTON'S LAW

The reason why a rocket is thrust upwards when fuel is burned is explained by the scientist Isaac Newton's famous third law of motion. He stated that for every action there is an equal and opposite reaction. So the action of the thrust upwards must be equal to the action of the exhaust downward.

Since the pressure in the combustion chamber is the same on all its parts, the pressure on the top is the same as the pressure that blows out the exhaust gases. It is this pressure that thrusts, or pushes, the rocket upwards.

A three-stage rocket has a number of fuel and oxygen tanks to provide all the fuel it needs.

Inventor's words

combustion
expand • expel
rocket • thrust

Make a balloon rocket

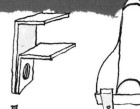

You will need

- panel of polystyrene
- white bendable card
- double-sided tape
- thick card
- stapler or strong glue
- 2 balloons
- plastic tubing
- black marker pen
- black and white paint
- paintbrush • string

1 Cut a base shape from polystyrene. With white bendable card and double-sided tape, make the body and wing tops of the rocket.

2 Make 2 rocket housing devices out of the thick card and staple or glue them on to the back of the rocket. Poke a hole into each.

3 Insert a balloon into each hole and secure with plastic tubing.

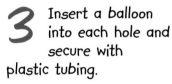

4 Decorate the rocket and glue on the tail piece.

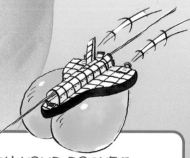

TO LAUNCH YOUR ROCKET

Thread string through the central section of the rocket and stretch it from one end of a room to the other, on a slope. Inflate the balloon engines, holding one while priming the other – and let fly!

How can I send many messages?

As telephones become cheaper, more and more people use them. Large numbers of calls are made at the same time. Ordinary telephone cables cannot cope with so many calls. A different kind of cable is needed to send thousands of signals at once.

Eli knows that a traditional telephone cable network does a good job. It transmits information that is made into a code, in the form of electrical pulses. The pulses are sent through electric wires. But with more and more calls being made, it is sometimes difficult to get through to his wife who works at the hospital.

The company where he works makes glass. It is trying to find a way to make cables that will carry more messages. But no one can figure out how electric pulses can travel through glass. It is not a substance that allows electricity to pass through.

How can the company make a new cable that carries more messages than the traditional one?

WHAT CAN IT DO?

- Perhaps it could make a glass cover for hundreds of electric cables. But the cable would be so fat, it would be too difficult to lay.

- What about making cables out of glass or using very thin glass fibres? But how would messages be sent along them?

- Maybe some kind of pulse other than electricity could be used. How about trying sound? Hmm, that doesn't work.

- The company could try pulses of light. But how could the pulses be made to stay in the glass cable?

We'll cover the very thin glass fibres with a covering, or cladding. A light source will feed the light into the fibre at one end. The cladding will end the light back inwards when it hits the inside of the fibre. A detector at the other end receives the light.

Each strand in a fibre optic cable carries pulses of light.

Coded messages

Fibre optics use a special way of sending messages. Fibre optic cables are long strands of special glass. They carry messages that are made up of pulses of light. Fibre optics can carry more messages than ordinary cables. In fibre optics communications systems, **lasers** – very strong beams of light – are used to feed the light into the fibres.

They transmit, or send, coded messages by flashing on and off at high speed. The messages travel through the fibres to devices that decode the messages and turn them back into the original signal. Fibre optics can carry messages from a few centimetres to 160km. The glass fibres in a fibre optic cable are less than 1mm thick.

Photons

A **photon** is a **particle**, a tiny speck of energy, that has been invented by scientists to explain how light behaves. Usually light behaves like waves, similar to the waves made when you throw something into a pool of water. But at other times, light seems to behave like a stream of tiny particles. These particles are called photons.

When an **atom** receives energy, the **electrons** in the atom soak up the energy and the atom becomes excited. The atom has to get back to normal, though, and to do this the electrons have to lose the energy they gained. They do this by squirting out the energy as photons, or bundles of light. All the colours of the light spectrum are given off as photons in this way. Photons of different coloured light have different amounts of energy. Photons of red light, for example, have less light than photons of violet light.

GLASS FIBRES

The tiny threads of glass called glass fibre can be used for many things, including optics. As they are flexible, they can be woven into cloth for fireproof clothing. They can also be used to make a plastic-like material called fibreglass.

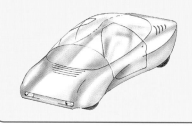

Computer-designed images of different photonic crystals materials that trap and give off light

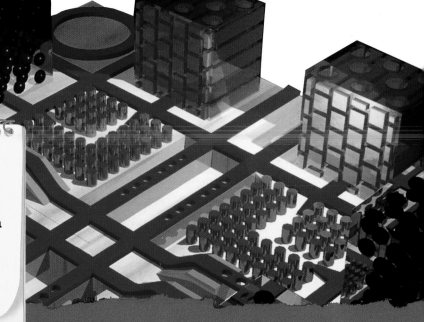

Inventor's words

atom • electron
fibre optics
laser • particle
photon

Make a fluorescent vase

You will need
- plastic bottle
- scissors
- string
- margarine tubs
- glow paints
- PVA glue
- brush

1 Cut a plastic bottle halfway down the neck. Cut notches around the rim and bend the flaps outwards to create the lip of the vase.

2 Cut several lengths of string. Soak each piece in a tub of glow paint. Take out and dry.

3 Brush glue all over the bottle. Now wind the pieces of string around the bottle, alternating the colours to make sizzling stripes.

4 You can make a collection of fluorescent string pots to hold glow sticks, glow straws or even a fibre optic torch!

Use metallic paints and glitter for a really jazzy display

How can we teach machines?

Some jobs are very boring and time-consuming. They require workers to do the same task over and over again, all day. Bosses think this is a waste of time and money, but what can take the place of the workers?

In the factory, Donald has to paint cars. When he has finished one, he starts another – and so it goes on.

Lee fixes on the doors. He never does anything else. Each one of the assembly line workers has one particular job to do.

How can we replace bored, expensive workers and still get the jobs done?

The managers have tried to make the jobs more interesting. They have even played music. But they wish there was some other way of doing these jobs where they didn't have to pay so many people.

WHAT CAN THEY DO?

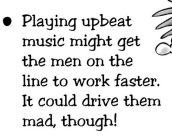

- Playing upbeat music might get the men on the line to work faster. It could drive them mad, though!

- How about putting the workers into a hypnotic trance so they wouldn't notice the time passing? But they'd still have to be paid.

- They could get a machine to do the work! But they'd need a man to work the machine.

- What if they devised a machine that had a brain, so that when it was taught to do a job, it wouldn't need a human to instruct it again?

New technology is the answer! A tiny computer can work as the robot's brain. Once it's been programmed – or taught – to do a job, the machine will do it without needing a human to work it.

Robot man, Electro, and Sparko, his dog, on display at the 1939 World Fair in New York.

Working robots

A **robot** is a machine that can do jobs without human help. Some robots are programmed to do repetitive tasks such as welding together steel panels to help make cars; others may do dangerous jobs inside nuclear reactors. The word 'robot' comes from the Czech word 'robota', which means 'hard work'.

A robot works by following a series of programmed instructions that tell it what has to be done to complete a job. These instructions are entered and stored in the robot's **control system**. The control system, either a computer or part of a computer, acts as a kind of electronic brain.

Robotics

Robotics is the science and technology that deals with the study and creation of robots. Robotics first involved creating machines that would do simple jobs such as painting or welding. But now, robotics scientists are trying to develop complex machines that can act almost like humans. It is unlikely, however, that robots that can think will ever be made.

Robotics technologists build robots of different sizes and designs, but few look anything like human beings. Most are machines that stay in one place and have one arm that is used for doing its job. But technologists are now developing more advanced robots that use television-type cameras for eyes and **electronic sensors** for touch. These robots act on feedback they get from their sensors rather than just stored instructions. These machines work like humans, but still cannot think like humans.

ROBO-PAINTER

Robots that paint cars have a control system that guides them as they work. The system's program tells the robot where to paint and for how long it must spray. But a robot cannot decide for itself what colour or pattern to paint.

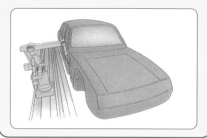

A robot removes a suitcase which may contain a bomb from a ca A video camera on top of the arm sends pictures to an operator watching at a safe distance.

Inventor's words

control system
electronic sensor
robot
robotics

Make your own robot

You will need

- plastic cake trays
- chocolate box trays
- large and small cartons
- toilet roll tubes
- plastic bottles • polystyrene
- PVA glue • chopsticks
- balloons, plastic ball, beads, marbles, bottle caps, sequins, stickers
- sticky tape • corrugated card
- egg-box • coat hanger wire
- kebab sticks
- silver spray paint

1 Make robot arms and legs out of plastic trays, cartons, polystyrene blocks or bottles glued together. Add wire tendons and make hands from egg box cartons.

2 Cut a window in a medium-sized carton. Stick a balloon, plastic ball, wires, beads and plastic moulding inside to make the robot's chest.

3 Cut a plastic bottle and a cardboard tube in half lengthwise. Glue on as shoulders and leg supports.

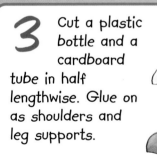

4 For the robot's head, stick bottle cap and marble eyes, cylindrical ears and a corrugated card mouth on to a small box. Use a toilet roll tube for the neck and attach to the shoulders.

5 Poke kebab sticks through the shoulders and hips, push on the polystyrene joints and attach the arms and legs. Spray with silver paint and decorate.

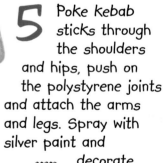
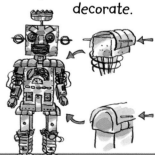

How can I make a powerful light?

Scientists are studying light and other kinds of radiation, or wave movement. Physicists have learned to make artificial radiation, such as microwaves, stronger. Very strong beams of radiation might be useful in the development of technology, industry and surgery.

Theodore knows about microwave amplification, or strengthening. The American physicist Charles Hard Townes has invented a device that demonstrates it. The device is called a maser. But Theodore is interested in other forms of radiation, especially light.

How can I make an beam of light so strong I could even cut with it?

During the 1950s, several people made designs for a device that amplifies light. But no one has built one yet. If only Theodore can actually build a light-amplifying device – he's sure it would have many uses.

WHAT CAN HE DO?

- Funnel a beam of sunlight through a series of increasingly thinner tubes?

- Look at the theories of Albert Einstein, who first suggested that radiation could be amplified?

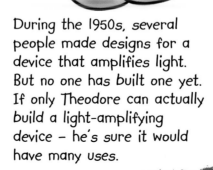

- Or study the ideas of the scientists Charles Townes and Arthur Schawlow, who explained how light from one source might stimulate light in another substance?

- If he focused a light on some kind of crystal, the atoms in it might become agitated and produce more light. But how would he direct the new light?

I could use a crystal of synthetic ruby in the shape of a tube. I'll put mirrors at each end to reflect light. Then I'll shine light at the crystal from a coil wrapped around it. The crystal will produce even stronger light as its atoms are agitated. The light will shoot out of one end in a thin beam.

Theodore Maiman with his first ruby laser in 1960. The crystal is cube-shaped.

Bright beam

A **laser** is a device that produces a fine, bright, powerful beam of light. It is made up of a crystal with a **flash tube**, a kind of flash bulb, coiled around it. There is a mirror at one end and a part mirror with a hole at the other. When light shines into the crystal, the **atoms** it is made up of become agitated, or move around more, and give off more energy in the form of light. This light is reflected by the mirrors at each end of the tube, making other atoms release light energy. The powerful light that has built up passes out of the tube as a laser beam. Lasers have many uses, including cutting body tissue in surgery, scanning bar codes and CDs, and as range finders in weapons.

One colour

Laser light is a fine beam of very strong light. It is different from ordinary light because it has low divergence, or spread, and it is onochromatic, which means it is made up of just one colour.

Most light spreads out very quickly. Light from a torch, for instance, spreads out, covers a large area and fades after just a short distance. Laser light moves in a much narrower beam and spreads out very little, even over long distances.

HOLOGRAM

A hologram is a special kind of photograph created by a laser. Because the image is three-dimensional, it looks as if it is solid. If you look at a hologram image from different positions, you see different views of it - just as you would of a solid object.

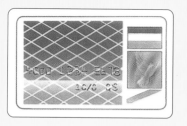

Light is made up of **electromagnetic waves** and each colour has a specific wave length, the length between the peaks of each wave. Ordinary light is made up of a number of wavelengths and colours, and appears as white light. Laser light is made up of waves with very narrow wavelengths, so it appears as a single colour.

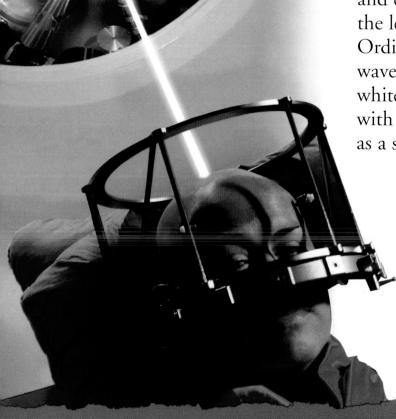

In a PET scanner, a laser beam connects the machine to the part of the body being examined.

Inventor's words

atom
divergence
electromagnetic
waves
flash tube • laser
monochromatic

Make a puppet theatre

You will need

- shoe box lid or cardboard box top
- scissors or craft knife
- cardboard
- thin paper or tracing paper
- stickers
- pieces of fabric
- black card
- kebab sticks • torch

1 Cut a hole for the screen in the centre of a shoe box lid. Next, cut a long strip of cardboard and make a back. Cut a slit on either side in which to slot stick puppets.

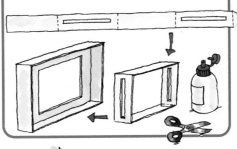

2 Fold a piece of cardboard into a cone shape and attach to the back to form a light chamber. Leave a hole at the far end in which to shine a torch.

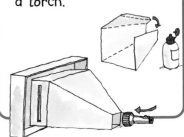

3 Stick a sheet of thin paper over the front hole to make a screen. Paint and decorate the box and add fabric curtains.

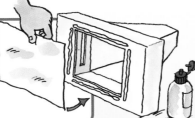

4 Make puppet characters from black card and tape to kebab sticks.

5 Push your puppets through the side slots, turn on the torch – and let the show begin!

Glossary and index

Aeroplane Heavier-than-air machine that travels through the atmosphere. It has an engine for power and wings to lift it into the air. p.17, 18

Atom Tiny part of an element, or simple substance, made up of an electron or electrons that move around a nucleus. The nucleus is made up of neutrons and protons. All the atoms in an element are identical. p.14, 22, 41

Automobile Road vehicle usually powered by an internal combustion. Some models are powered by electricity or have dual power systems. p.5

Combustion When a substance combines with oxygen and is heated, it combusts, or burns. p.30

Combustion engine Engine that uses burning and the fast expansion of gases to create power. A petrol-burning engine is a combustion engine. p.5

Control system Electronic system that controls the actions of a machine. p.37, 38

Cylinder Solid shape with two ends that are flat and circular. In a machine, it is a hollow tube with a piston moving up and down inside. p.5

Diaphragm Thin, flat sheet of material. Electric signals make the diaphragm inside a telephone vibrate. p.13

Divergence Two lines spreading out in different directions from the same point. p.42

Electromagnetic waves Waves of radiation including light, radio, X-rays and gamma rays that make up the electromagnetic spectrum. p.42

Electron Tiny speck of matter that is usually part of an atom. An electron moves in an orbit around the nucleus of an atom. p.14, 22

Electron gun Device found inside a television set or electron microscope. It uses electricity to fire a beam of electrons at a special screen. p.22

Electronic sensor Device that picks up, or senses, electrical impulses or signals so they can be examined. p.38

Element Simple substance, either a solid, liquid or gas, that contains the same kind of atoms. There are about 100 kinds of natural elements and a few artificial ones. p.26

Expand Become bigger or take up more space. Most gases, liquids and solids expand when they are heated. p.29

Expel Push or drive out by force. p.30

Fibre optics Fibre optic cables are long strands of special glass. They carry messages made up of pulses of light. Fibre optics can carry more messages than ordinary cables. p.33

Flash tube Type of flashbulb that is coiled around a laser tube. It provides light for the laser tube. p.41

Fossil fuel Type of fuel that comes from solids, liquids or gases under the ground. Fossil fuels were formed millions of years ago from buried plants and animals. p.6

Foundations The part of a building located at its base to stabilise it. Some foundations are flat while others are dug into the ground. p.9, 10

Four-stroke engine Type of internal combustion engine. Each of the four strokes is an up or down movement of a piston inside the engine. p.5

Frame The part of a building that acts as a kind of skeleton to its weight. It is made of steel or concrete p.9

Girder Steel bar used in buildings as part of the frame. p.9

Iconoscope Type of electronic television camera created by Russian Vladimir Zworykin. p.21

Insulator Substance that does not allow the flow of heat or electricity through it. Plastic coverings act as insulators on copper wires. p.26

Integrated circuit Tiny electric circuit that can be fitted into small devices such as computers or calculators. Also called a microchip. p.25

Kinescope Early version of the television picture tube invented by Russian Vladimir Zworykin. p.21

Laser Device that produces beam of very strong and powerful light. Lasers are used in medicine, industry and for entertainment. p.33, 41, 42

Load Weight that a force pushes against. Machines move loads, while beams support them. p.9, 10

Monochromatic Shades of black and white. A black-and-white photograph is monochromatic. p.42

Neutron A tiny particle of matter found at the nucleus of an atom. A neutron has no electrical charge. p.14

Matter Everything in the universe that occupies space and has weight. Matter can be a solid, liquid or gas. p.14

Nucleus Centre of an atom, containing protons and neutrons. p.14

Particle Tiny piece of matter such as an electron or an atom. p.14, 22, 34

Petrol Type of fossil fuel. p.5, 6

Phosphor Type of solid used to coat the inside of cathode ray tubes. Phosphors give off light when hit by electrons. p.22

Phosphorescent An object is phosphorescent when the phosphors on it glow. p.22

Photon Particle of light. Scientists use this word to describe light when it behaves like a stream of particles rather than a wave. p.34

Piston Tube-like device that fits snugly into a cylinder and moves up and down or backwards and forwards. Pistons are used in internal combustion engines and pumps. p. 5

Propeller Ships and some aeroplanes use propellers to generate force. A propeller has two or more plates called blades that are joined to a shaft. The shaft and blades are turned by an engine.   p.17

Proton Tiny particle of matter that is found in the nucleus of an atom. A proton has a positive electric charge.   p.14

Refinery Type of factory where oil is refined, or broken down, into various substances such as petrol, grease and paraffin.   p.6

Robot Machine that can do jobs without human help. It can be programmed to do boring or dangerous jobs, but it cannot make decisions on its own.   p.37, 38

Robotics Science of creating and building robots.   p.38

Rocket Powerful engine that uses a mixture of fuel and oxygen to produce gas at high pressure. The gas is expelled at great force, which thrusts the engine forward. A spacecraft that uses this type of engine is also called a rocket.   p.29, 30

Semiconductor Substance such as silicon that can be treated to carry an electric current. Semiconductors do not conduct currents as well as conductors do.   p.26

Silicon Grey-coloured chemical element. It is used to make integrated circuits because it can act as a semiconductor. p.26

Silicon chip Integrated circuit printed on a thin wafer of silicon.   p.25, 26

Skyscraper Very tall building with many storeys, or levels.   p.9, 10

Superstructure Part of a skyscraper that is above ground.   p.9

Telephone Device for communicating over a distance, or out of the hearing range of another person. It has a mouthpiece for turning sound waves into electronic signals, and an earpiece that turns the signals back into sound.   p.13, 14

Television Method of sending and receiving sounds and pictures over a distance. It uses radio waves to carry electric signals through the atmosphere.   p.21, 22

Thrust Push created by a force. Thrust is created in a rocket by the force of rapidly expanding gas.   p.17, 29

Wing Projecting parts of an aeroplane that create lift. Wings are shaped so that the top side is longer than the bottom side. This creates less pressure on top and a push, or lift, underneath.   p.18

Tools and Materials

Almost all of the materials in this book can be found around the house or bought at your local art or craft shop. If you cannot find the exact item, try and replace it with something similar.

Most of the models will stick fast with PVA glue or even wallpaper paste. However, some materials need a stronger glue so take care when using these as they may damage your clothes and even your skin. Ask an adult to help you.

Always protect furniture with newspaper or a large cloth, and cover your clothes by wearing an apron.

User Care

Take special care when handling sharp tools such as scissors, pointed gadgets, pieces of wire or craft knives. Ask an adult to help you when you need to use them.